BODY AND SOUL

About the author

As well as twelve previous collections of poetry, Anthony Cronin has written a number of admired prose works, including biographies of Flann O'Brien and Samuel Beckett; collections of essays; the classic memoir of Dublin in the 1950s, *Dead as Doornails*; and novels including *The Life of Riley*, which has recently been reissued by New Island Books in the Modern Irish Classics series.

Born in Enniscorthy, he is married to the writer Anne Haverty and lives in Dublin. He is a founding member of Aosdána, of which he was made a Saoi in 2003, a distinction conferred for exceptional artistic achievement.

Body

and

Soul

Anthony Cronin

NEW ISLAND

BODY AND SOUL
First published 2014
by New Island Books
16 Priory Hall Office Park
Stillorgan
County Dublin

www.newisland.ie

PRINT ISBN: 978-1-84840-399-4
EPUB ISBN: 978-1-84840-401-4
MOBI ISBN: 978-1-84840-400-7

British Library Cataloguing Data. A CIP catalogue record for this book
is available from the British Library

Typeset by Mariel Deegan & New Island
Cover design by Mariel Deegan & New Island
Printed by SPRINT-print Ltd.

New Island receives financial assistance from
The Arts Council (An Chomhairle Ealaíon),
70 Merrion Square, Dublin 2, Ireland).

10 9 8 7 6 5 4 3 2 1

For Donal Lunny,
friend, and friend to poetry.

Praise for Anthony Cronin

'Anthony Cronin's *The Fall* has marvellous poems in it which are formally perfect, wise, surprising, filled with dark knowledge and animated by a glittering mind.'

– Colm Toibin, *The Irish Times*

'Above all he is a lover of life, a friend to women and the young... Despite his disabused – i.e. realistic – take on the world, he can't help being in love with it and its radiance of magic moments on windy cliff or in sunlit garden... And despite a brisk refusal of sentimentality there is a delicate wholeheartedness throughout... He tells no lies. This is the real world; we live in history. He wouldn't want to be considered a 'national poet' (we have several) but in a certain way he is, albeit a contrarian one. The comparison, *mutatis mutandis*, might be with Pablo Neruda of Chile, who also saw poetry and politics as part of the same activity. He too has spent thoughtful hours on the heights of Machu Picchu, though we call them the Cliffs of Moher.'

– Derek Mahon, *An Unflinching Gaze, Selected Prose*

'Cronin is a major voice; he is Ireland's modern-day Dryden, a master of the public word in the public place.'

– George Szirtes

Table of Contents

The Lesser Yellow Celandine

When the Lesser Yellow Celandine
Took William Wordsworth's eye
English poets soon began
To think they had to try

To find on walks past coppices,
In dingles, dells and nooks
Flowers for reflection on
In their poetic books.

And even Irish poets sought
Among thistles, ragwort, dock,
In boggy fields and bouldered,
Among droppings of the flock,

The same illumination
The old sharp-shooter found
(Or was it consolation?)
As he went upon his round

In his white stock, black stockings
And serviceable shoes
(His serviceable greatness too
Easing so many woes).

But the flowers of the handbook
Are in Ireland hard to find
Though you search among the sceachs and thorns
Until you think you're blind,

And nature's subjects generally
Are shy, retiring, rare,
Retreating from the human gaze
As does the Kerry hare.

While some most famous fauna
Are chimeras that we know
Mostly from English literature,
A rich source of such woe.

Where are the munching moles that eat
Old England in their excavation
And solve by way of shapely mounds
The problem of its defecation?

Where are the nightingales that sob
Superbly in each bush
On moonlit nights at midnight in
A wide and starry hush?

Yes, Ireland is a poorish place,
Few poorer to be found,
And much of nature shuns it as
Unprofitable ground.

Nikolaus Nikolayevich

Nikolaus Nikolayevich was killing himself,
But he said he was not afraid.
No one could be afraid of death
Who has endured this life, he said...

Does the east wind cut you in half there
Or the treachery of a friend?
Do you shiver under the bridge there
Awake or asleep at the end?

He gulped from his vodka bottle,
Making his Adam's apple swerve,
I suppose it could be quicker, he said,
But I haven't got the nerve.

Nor could I defy the Creator like that
Although I owe him small thanks.
When I was a lad it was the ultimate sin,
Far beyond lies and wanks.

And the vodka's good for a while, he went on,
Watching the wavering snow fall
From under the roof of the railway shed,
Becoming the world's white pall.

The Madness of Mammon

When Mammon finally went mad
And refused to leave the inner palace
His priests decided the people were so docile
That everything could still go on as before.
And so priests and people chanted together:

The sins of the rich shall be visited on the poor.
The poorer we are, the more honest we are required to be.
Monetary value is the only value.
Education is a means to self-advancement.
You do not work to live. You live to work.
The expression 'wasting time' is obsolete,
There is only the problem of passing it.
Work is the best way of passing the time.
If we all work for less,
Then we can all have work.

And as the people happily chanted
The priests smiled with satisfaction,
Staring into Mammon's glassy insane eyes.
Everything will be as before,
They told him, there is nothing to fear.

Endangered Species

Say goodbye to the Bengal Tiger,
'Cheerio,' to the Polar Bear,
The next time you muse upon either
It may very well not be there.

And spare a wave for the Walrus,
Perched on a rock in the sea,
A great, fat, flipper-legged fellow,
Who has almost ceased to be.

Not to mention the Scarlet Macaw
Which can live to be sixty-five,
And be put in a cage to say 'How do you do?'
If it's lucky enough to survive.

And before very long the Elephant,
The philosopher of the wild,
Will only exist in the zoo or circus,
Patient, sapient, mild.

And the Wild Asses of Africa
Who stamped their hooves on the ground
Before King Solomon met his queen
May be nowhere to be found.

Nor the Bird of Paradise, so named
Because only heavenly birth
Could account for a plumage so lovely
That it had no place on our earth.

The Life of Man

All that excitement, all that fear and pain
And then snuff out and never be again?

Talking

Talking? You say six sentences.
And you have at least three reasons
For remorse or regret.

Silent, you brood on your foolishness.
You resolve to say nothing.
Careless asserters, inaccurate gossipers
And the plainly malicious
Will go uncorrected.

You brood on your silence.
Why do I not speak up?
Can I not speak moderately
In measured, sensible, judicious tones?

But this is no time for the measured.
Everybody is floating on a tide
Of inspiration, malice, wrong
Information, misplaced enthusiasm.

So you launch in.
You send yourself.
You are possessed by the *hwyl*.
In a few minutes, one
Major regret, two minor.

You brood on your rashnesses.

Shining Through

When Dickens described faces,
Especially young girls' faces
He would sometimes say the soul
Shone through them.

But all our souls are lost souls now.
They have wandered off,
Over the yellow foam.
Even the souls of the young girls
Dickens didn't worry about,
As he strolled down to the brothel
With his old pal Wilkie Collins.

When you drop into a gathering now
What comes shining through
Even a young girl's face
Is the worry of an anxious ego,
Self-centred, self-absorbed,
Fearful of being overlooked.
When you go to a party
You meet a mob of egos,
Some silently murderous.

The Supreme Commandment

In Aramaic or whatever,
He commanded us to love one another.
In Aramaic, or anything else
It is a tall order.

Many get the love
Knocked out of them early.
Outside the family
(Which isn't always loving
Either, but that's another story)
It's a world of bullying, fear
And commonplace cruelty.

And everybody has to live.
And has to be tough with others,
Writing brutal letters
For their boss's gain,
About mortgages and evictions,
Forbidden to forgive,
Suppressing mercy,
Closing off pain.

If he had said 'like'?
You have to like one another.
Well, so what?
Most of us like quite a few
Though when they are in trouble,
We say, there's nothing I can do.

'Tolerate' might have been
The lesson to inculcate.
In Aramaic or whatever,
You must learn to tolerate
Others, their habits,
Their hurtful sayings,
Their unattractive faces,
Their little betrayings,
As you tolerate your own.
We all look in the mirror.
We are all well-practised
In difficult cases.

Blessings

Once upon a time,
There were many holy men here.
(Women could not really be holy,
Though they could be pious.)

And these grave, holy men
Gave freely of their holiness,
Blessing many things with two fingers
Of their raised hands.

Almost everything you could think of,
Almost everywhere you could go
Had been blessed by the holy men
With the two fingers.

They blessed dance halls.
Hurling-matches, hostelries, houses.
'Bless this house, Oh Lord, I pray,
Keep it safe
By night and day',
John McCormick sang
On the homely radio.

Nowadays he would have to add,
'From the banks'
But no matter, people
Nowadays would laugh at the idea
Of a blessing
Saving anything from harm.

Nothing in this fair land
Will ever be blessed again.

A Recession

The earth remained:
Patient, forbearing
Willing to yield as always.
The sun was punctual to the same appointments
With the great grain-bearing plains,
The seas waited to give up their dripping silver netfuls.
The black men went
To choke underground
While they tore out the rock
That kept white men rich.
There had been no reduction
In the fruitfulness
And fertility of the world.

But even in the rich countries,
Even among what were called the middle-classes
Let alone among those already hard-pressed,
There was sudden poverty and want.
Wages were reduced, pensions wiped out.
Many went hungry. There were no jobs
And nothing much to hope for.
Experts argued, blaming this or that.
They called it a recession,
Implying that it was somehow natural, endemic,
Beyond our control,
Like an earthquake or a flood.

But it wasn't.

This was man-made,
Made by market manipulation,
Human greed, debt exploitation,
Spurning the goodness of the willing earth.
And while the once bright streets
Showed fading colours, gaps, and empty buildings
Dark limousines
Slipped purposefully through them,
White yachts lapped
Happily at sunlit quaysides
And slender jet-planes confirmed the existence
Of parallel lives full of ambition, eagerness, avarice.

God

He came down to the vast river.
There were thousands in the water,
Chanting, screaming, venting their delight.
It was as noisy as a football match.
The water was a creamy brown
From the excrement of the animals
That had been brought there
To share the river's goodness
And there were tumbling carcasses
Because upstream
There had been a mighty flood.
After submerging himself totally
He came up between two drowned cows,
Their bellies ballooned with gas.

He was full of joy.
God was everywhere, it
Was all God.

Forgiveness

The Reverend Ian Paisley,
A muffled, fog-bound voice from other days,
Suddenly says again
That the Pope is Antichrist.
Why? Because he pretends
To be able to forgive us our sins.
Only Christ, the Reverend insists,
Can forgive anyone their sins.

He does not know that Christ
Lost the power to forgive us our sins
One summer night in Geneva
Two hundred years ago
Beneath unblinking stars.

No-one, no power in heaven or earth
Can forgive anyone their sins now
Except those they have sinned against.
And if they are dead and gone
The sins must remain unforgiven
Now and forever.

Body and Soul

Marriages between bodies and souls
Were once indissoluble.
There was no divorce, no separation,
No annulment.

And the two were often very close,
Going everywhere together.
Of course the body appeared
To be the busier, while the soul
Seemed to spend much of its time pottering,
Sitting reading at the kitchen table
Beside the oil-lamp,
Ruminating.

But in fact it had a job.
While the body toiled and moiled
It aspired.
That was its task:
Aspiration.

When the body,
Sweaty, lustful, prone to infections
In dubious places,
Probably as a result of dubious activities,
Dragged things down
Into the mire and fever.
The soul tried to raise them up.
It wanted both of them to long
For the same thing, which was

Higher.
But from the soul's point of view
The principal snag
In this tug-of-war
Was that the body nearly always won –
Not just 'yielded to temptation'
But found the whole corporeal
Immediate world, with its tradings,
Its pressures, its politics,
Its economics, its sport, such an
Interesting complex place to be
That it had no time for what the soul
Wanted. And even the people
Who weren't enjoying the ordinary
World, with its wants and needs,
Its loyalties and treacheries,
Found it so absorbing, so
Deserving of all their attention,
That the soul became a nuisance,
An unwelcome hanger-on,
Apologetic, hang-dog, over-anxious,
Languishing when the subject of who would get
The Brussels job,
Or win the World Cup, was discussed.
Making it plain when these topics
Came up, that it had an acute
Longing for something
Higher.

For a while people had
These awkward souls,
Whingeing, pleading, reproaching,
Miserably keeping company with them.
But because they were so un-appreciated
Both by the body to which they were attached
And by their friends,
Many souls started to stay at home
And became depressed,
No longer pretending to take an interest
In what went on in the Dáil,
Or the Senate, or the Law Courts.
Some were such a nuisance
That their partners preferred them
To stay at home, rather than spoil
The talk at the dinner-party.

And so these marriages of soul and body
Fell apart, and the government
Changed the law.
Such marriages were no longer indissoluble.
Divorce between body and soul was possible.
Even annulment.

So you encounter few souls now,
In the world most of us live in
Most of the time
And people
Are more or less right when they say,
'It is a soulless place'.

Impossibilities

They advocated the utterly impossible,
The great ones just gone,
Asked that we buck the tide of our time
For causes both silly and forlorn.

When everything was intentionally debased,
Yeats wanted the noble to be a subject for contemplation.
And even, should the circumstance demand,
A stance for imitation.

While capitalism's tentacles tightened their grip
Even in the remotest land,
Pound preached in poetry an economics that
Few could understand.

During an era of unequalled cliché and platitude,
The poetic purification
Of the dialect of the tribe
Was Eliot's recommendation.

On these grave subjects they were bound to look foolish
However wisely they might otherwise write.
For on these grave subjects the children of darkness
Are wiser in their generation than the children of light.

After Thomas Moore

Dear harp of my country, in Celtness I found thee,
The chain of Antiqueness had hung o'er thee long,
When proudly, my own island harp, I unbound thee,
And gave all thy chords to the street and its song.

Memories of a Lifetime

There are those nowadays who are
The vendors of wonderful memories
Of which you can avail,
Who know how to create them
And have them for immediate sale.
'The memory of a lifetime!'
'Acquire these wonderful memories!'
'Let us make memories for you to treasure!'
'Create memories for the years to come!'

But remembering, alas,
Is not always such a pleasure.
Even the memory of that Greek cruise,
A short self-contained interlude
Comparatively free from booze,
May not be entirely scant of things
Best left not remembered
And realisations
Best not borne in on you.

And the memory and
The experience are different things
Which only laborious art
Could synthesise.
The memory, without the hearing,
The smell, taste or touch,
Is of the past.
Even if it was a happy time
It did not last.

Everything has changed
Or has fallen apart.
The cruise in the Aegean
Is over, and the thought
Of it a stab to the heart.

And in any time, in
Any relationship,
There were failures,
Things said,
Things left unsaid. Trivia
Maybe – but as they swim
To the surface of memory
They do not seem
Trivial, especially if they involve
Our most powerful concern:
Our self-esteem.

So beware of the memories
You book,
Ask for guarantees
That they will be ones with which
You will be glad to be stuck.

Community Spirit

In times of disaster they praise us
For the community spirit we show.
They're enthusiastic about it
On the radio.

When we pulled an old lady
Through the window of her flooded abode
And put her in a boat outside
It was community spirit we showed.

When she floated down to the schoolhouse
And was given a cup of tea
This too was welcomed as proof
Of community.

But when the flood subsides
And it's back to normal once more,
When the old lady recovers
The use of her own door,

They say, 'Prosperity
Doesn't come from that community stuff.
It comes from competition,
Keen, ruthless and rough.

If she can't pay the bill
For the electricity
The let her do without
Her encouraging cups of tea.'

Final

We could count on quarrels,
Expect estrangements,
But the past would never be final.
It would never be a history
Written in stone, while, at the same time, incomplete.

There would always be another chapter,
One in which you could explain,
Write a letter,
Make that telephone call,
Send that message,
Unify it all.

Spring

And we had waited for the Spring so long,
Peering, examining every branch,
Questioning, comparing the months and years.

But suddenly Spring was everywhere,
Indubitable buds, shining cream-white blossom,
Dock leaves behind the wheelie bins.
A green mist among branches
And through a window, evening light.

But anyway, we said then, Spring
Will come again next year.
And maybe next year, bring us what we seek.

Adam Expelled

I could see the undying rose from where I stood,
God's rose; and therefore destined to bloom on
In calm perfection while the ones I planted
Died of mere time, of mere mortality;
See its plot too, cropped and mowed and measured
By the mowers and dividers in God's mind.
Unlike the tangled matted space I cleared
With such repeated drudgery to plant
My own bedraggled, blighted little bush.
Well, God has said that labour will be torment
And possibly he meant
Not just the pains, discomforts
Of actual toil, the bending, stretching, pulling,
But something now inevitable here;
The disappointed hope
Of such green ground, such perfect
Sheathed rose-buds.

Of course I know with what of reason's left,
It is impossible to emulate him and overcome
The imperfections, now our mode of being.
I know I'll never see
The perfect rose unless
While standing in a favoured spot, I catch
Such glimpse of God's;
As merely tortures me.

But then illusion, one more gift or curse
Which we, who were once the clear-eyed,

Were given when we left to ease, or even
Further blight this mortal state –
Ambiguous, you see, like all his gifts –
May well in time work magic with my rose.
Illusion is a comfort to our being
But also it's a weapon in our world –
As my sons know, whose sadly vicious quarrels,
Feeding on misery's
Induced imaginings
Would be impossible without it.

Perhaps deliberately foregoing
Such glimpses of God's rose as I might get,
Wrapping myself, which I could easily do
In this provided cloak
Of coaxed illusion,
Forgetting, which I gradually could,
There was another rose, in time I might
Deceive myself enough
To think perfection
Not now and here impossible and even
That my own scraggy, loose-leaved flower attained it.

Of course the thought is sad but the attainment
Could easily be happy beyond measure.
For what is happiness but being well-deceived?
That may be all which we can hope for now

This side of his great barrier,
This side of angels
With their flaming swords.

A Spiritual People

The Irish go on pilgrimage
To Santiago now.
They like the sunlit walk
Which is good for the health.

When they went on pilgrimage before
It was nearly always to some place
Where the bitter wet wind
Blew from the north-east,
And where, sustained only
By hunks of stale dry bread
And mugfuls of strong black tea,
They crouched all night
Awake among the rocks
Reciting the Sorrowful Mysteries.

The misery of it all
Was presumed to show their spirituality
As was the intensity with which they prayed
For what was uppermost in their anxious,
Often desperate hearts –

That Daddy would give up the drink,
That Aunt May would be cured
Of the sciatica,
That Jim would pass the exam and become
A permanent and pensionable
Civil servant.
They prayed too that they might get
An uncle's farm,
A corporation house,

A man,
A woman,
That lovely coat in Monica Dowd's
In time for Statia's wedding,
Their new teeth done in time
For Statia's wedding.

Even on the road to Santiago
We do not pray so much now,
Having lost our faith
In the all-powerful Father
Who could change things at a nod,
And in the loving Mother
Who never refused
To ask him,
And to whom he always listened.

But if we did still pray
For what was uppermost
In our anxious, sometimes
Desperate hearts
That you might think were beating
Their wings
Against the bars of the temporal,
It would belong to the temporal,
Not the spiritual world.

The temporal is our sphere,
We know no other.
Whatever walls and halls it may have
We are condemned to our temporal yearnings,
For Statia's wedding
And the coat in Monica Dowd's.

New poetry available from New Island Books:

The Venice Suite
Dermot Bolger

*'A sequence of poems that no writer would
ever wish to write ...'.*

Written in the aftermath of the death of his wife in
2010, The Venice Suite is a deeply personal sequence
of poems that charts the author's experience of sudden
bereavement. It explores the stages and states of loss in
an irrevocably altered world, where one partner is left
behind to deal with the ongoing business of living
while trying to comprehend the enormity of the
severance of a shared life suddenly rendered into the
past tense. They manage to be richly tender love poems
while trying to map the unknown new territory in
which any bereaved person finds themselves.

*'The memories contained here are unique to me,
yet the voyage of loss it tries to chart is undertaken
by thousands of people every year ...'.*
— Dermot Bolger

About the author:
Born in Dublin in 1959, Dermot Bolger is a poet,
novelist and playwright, whose novels include *The
Journey Home*; *The Woman's Daughter*; *The Valparaiso
Voyage* and *The Family on Paradise Pier*. His most
recent books are his collection of plays, *The Ballymun
Trilogy*, his young adult novel, *New Town Soul*, and his
novella, *The Fall of Ireland*.

Dream Country
Donna Sørensen

A sublime and original collection of poetry from a talented and exciting new voice.

In this, her début collection of poems, writer Donna Sørensen explores a wide range of ideas that are thematically connected by a common thread: the idea of home – what it first appears to be, what it really is and why it matters. Challenging traditional notions of one's home and place, Sørensen, who has lived outside her native land for over a decade, finds that 'home' can be a matter of what we carry with us rather than where we take it, can be a feeling rather than a belief, and can exist in connections with people and ideas rather than objects and places.

About the author:
Donna Sørensen was born and raised in the UK, but has been living outside it since 2006. She spent three years living and working in Ireland, where her poetry has been published in journals such as *Poetry Ireland Review, Southword, Cyphers, THE SHOp, Crannóg, Revival, Wordlegs* and *The Bare Hands Anthology*. She has also been published in *Orbis* (UK). Donna was selected to read at the Poetry Ireland Introductions Series 2011 and at the Cork Spring Poetry Festival 2012. She appeared as *The Stinging Fly*'s Featured Poet in the Spring 2012 issue. A version of this collection received a commendation in the 2011 Patrick Kavanagh Poetry Award. She now lives in Copenhagen, Denmark.

Collected Poems
Anthony Cronin

Anthony Cronin's *Collected Poems* brings together the work of a poetic lifetime by this celebrated Irish poet, from his first book, published in London in 1957, to this collection, published by New Island Books in 1999, as well as a number of new poems. This landmark collection displays Cronin's innate lyrical gift, his honesty to human experience, his range, his always immanent humour and sheer poetic intelligence.

Collected Poems, comprehensive and authoritative, also brings together the longer compositions that have been a notable part of his poetic practice – from *RMS Titanic*, described by Paul Durcan as 'a major work', to *The End of the Modern World*, which Anthony Burgess declared 'should be as well known as *The Wasteland*'.

In its depth, eloquence and poetic power, *Collected Poems* will surprise even Anthony Cronin's most fervent admirers.

'We need him. Not a poet in Ireland should feel confident he is better.'
— James Simmons

'Cronin is one of our finest and most dedicated poets, his work stretching back more than fifty years ... his warm commitment and tenacious artistry remind us of the supreme value of the enterprise.'
— Derek Mahon

Selected Poems: Rogha Dánta
Nuala Ní Dhomhnáill

First published in 1988, *Selected Poems: Rogha Dánta*
by Nuala Ní Dhomhnaill, with translations by Michael
Hartnett, played a major role in bridging the historical
divide between Irish poets writing in Irish and those
writing in English. At the same time, these poems –
drawn from folklore, dream and mythology, yet giving
voice to an utterly new world – helped to copperfasten
Nuala Ní Dhomhnaill's reputation as one of Ireland's
foremost poets, irrespective of language or gender.

Reissued by New Island Books with a new afterword
by the author, *Selected Poems: Rogha Dánta* remains a
landmark text in Irish poetry publishing.

> *'Nuala's Irish is like that of children brought up by
> their grandmothers, a hundred years old, a kind of
> miracle of survival. I can only say that I hear the
> tribe speaking through her . . . Her talent is profound
> and exuberant; her command of the medium
> absolute.'*

> – Máire Mhac an tSaoi

Poppy's Leavetaking
Tom Mac Intyre

'The words are all that matter ... Mac Intyre's language becomes a route in and out of experience.'
– Gerard Dawe, *The Irish Times*

'Mac Intyre is a shaman. These are strange and beautiful poems from a strange and beautiful territory ...'
– Marina Carr

In this vibrant new collection, veteran writer Tom Mac Intyre embraces life with vigour, his poetry resonating with his trademark imagery, humour, presence and power. Alive to the sublime in the simple and the everyday, his words uncover the beauty and simplicity in the world that our eyes so often miss.

About the author:
Tom Mac Intyre was born in 1931 in Cavan, where he still lives. A dual-language writer, he has written several books of poetry as well as many plays for the Abbey Theatre (Peacock Stage). Amongst his short fiction is *Find the Lady* (New Island Books, 2008), *The Harper's Turn* (with an introduction by Seamus Heaney) and *The Word for Yes: New and Selected Stories*. His poetry collections include *ABC: New Poems* (New Island Books, 2006) and, most recently, *Encountering Zoe* (New Island Books, 2010). He is a member of Aosdána.

An Arid Season: New Poems
President Michael D. Higgins

Michael D. Higgins's *An Arid Season: New Poems* is the distillation of over ten years' work. Inspiring and evocative, this long-awaited new collection is reflective of the changes that were taking place, not just in the poet's life, but also in the world at large.

'It was a time,' says the poet, 'when I often felt that language was losing its meaning. Life was being commodified in all its aspects; values seemed out of fashion.'

Discerning a residual hunger for the spiritual, Michael D. Higgins probes our collective consciousness, investigating the nature of memory and of prophecy, exploring both our imagined and realised worlds.

> *'The salt of tears is a deposit in memory of our sea beginnings:*
> *there is lodged the long sigh of all our time, lost in endless space.'*
>
> – Michael D. Higgins

Also by Anthony Cronin,
and available from New Island Books:

The Life of Riley
Anthony Cronin

'A comic triumph'
— The New York Times

The Life of Riley is at once a comic masterpiece and a tragic accout of one man's wilful descent into a glorious life of beggardom. Having left his job as Assistant to the Secretary of the Irish Grocers' Association, Riley is free to spend his days and nights perfecting the art of blagging a drink at O'Turks pub, unimpeded by responsibility.

A masterful portrait of the Irish at hime and abroad, *The Life of Riley* will take you sauntering through Dublin streets and slums, London pubs and labour exchanges in the company of a vibrant cast of misfit characters.

'I have laughed more at The Life of Riley *than at any other book I have ever read.'*
— Benedict Kiely, The Irish Times

'Gorgeously funny … True, crude, raw, rude, nude.'
— Elizabeth Smart, Queen

'A splendidly comic imagination'
— The Times Literary Supplement